How Does Weather Change?

by Jennifer Boothroyd

first step nonfiction

Lerner Publications Company · Minneapolis

LERNER

Expand learning beyond the printed book. Download free, complementary educational resources for this book from our website, www.lerneresource.com.

SOURCE™

The images in this book are used with the permission of: © Stuart Monk/Shutterstock.com, p. 4; © Hermera/Thinkstock, p. 5; © iStockphoto.com/Mari, p. 6; © Donna Smith Photography/Shutterstock.com, p. 7; © Hallgerd/Shutterstock.com, p. 8; © Photobank gallery/Shutterstock.com, p. 9; © David Kay/Shutterstock.com, p. 10; © TSpider/Shutterstock.com, p.11; © iStockphoto.com/skynesher, p. 12; © Thomas Gordon/Getty Images, p. 13; © Sunny Forest/Shutterstock.com, p. 14; © Samuel Borges/Shutterstock.com, p. 15; © Edyta Linek/Dreamstime.com, p. 16; © Shelli Jensen/Shutterstock.com, p. 17; © Galushko Sergey/Shutterstock.com, p. 18; © Goodshoot/Thinkstock, p. 19; © Maryna Pleshkun/Shutterstock.com, p. 19; © iStockphoto.com/ideabug, p. 20; © iStockphoto.com/ktaylorg, p. 21; © Olesia Bilkei/Shutterstock.com, p. 22.

Front cover: © Markus Gann/Shutterstock.com

Main body text set in ITC Avant Garde Gothic Std Medium 21/25.
Typeface provided by Adobe Systems.

Lerner Publications Company
A division of Lerner Publishing Group, Inc.
241 First Avenue North
Minneapolis, MN 55401 USA

For reading levels and more information, look up this title at www.lernerbooks.com.

Library of Congress Cataloging-in-Publication Data

The Cataloging-in-Publication Data for How Does Weather Change? is on file at the Library of Congress.
ISBN: 978-1-4677-3917-7 (LB)
ISBN: 978-1-4677-4678-6 (EB)

Manufactured in the United States of America
1 – CG – 7/15/14

Table of Contents

Changes in the Air   4

Changes during the Day   13

Changes with the Seasons   17

Glossary   23

Index   24

Changes in the Air

It's a sunny day. Let's go play outside!

Oh no. What happened to the **weather**?

5

Bundle up if the weather gets cold!

Weather can change quickly.

Wind is moving this flag.

Wind makes weather change.

You can't
see wind.

Slow wind is called a
breeze.

A gust is a fast wind.

Wind moves **clouds** in the sky.

You can't see much sun through these clouds.

Clouds can block the sunshine.

Clouds make snow fall.

Clouds can bring **rain** or **snow**.

The air is cooler in the early morning.

The air warms up as the
sun rises.

The air is usually hottest in the early afternoon.

The air cools down as the sun goes down.

The weather changes with the **seasons**.

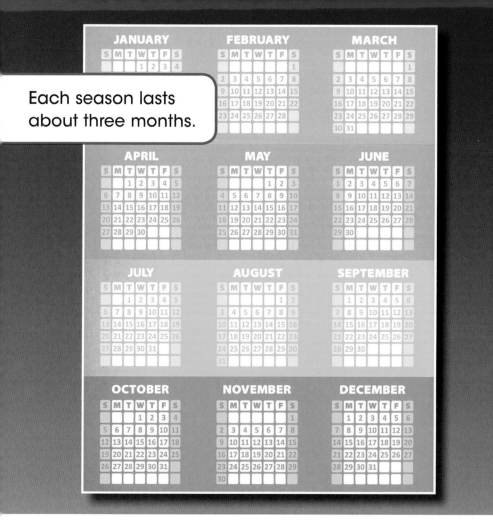

Each season lasts about three months.

There are four seasons in the year.

Summer weather is hot.

A hat helps
keep you warm.

Autumn weather is cooler.

Winter can be very cold.

Which season do you like best?

Spring weather is often rainy.

Glossary

clouds – groups of very tiny water drops floating in the sky

rain – water drops that fall from clouds

seasons – four different times of the year. The seasons are summer, autumn, winter, and spring.

snow – ice crystals that fall from clouds

weather – what happens in the outside air

wind – air moving around outside

Index

air – 13–16

clouds – 10–12

rain – 12, 22

seasons – 17–22

snow – 12

sunshine – 11

wind – 7–10